Both

Both

Steven Blyth

Published 2012 by
Smokestack Books
PO Box 408, Middlesbrough TS5 6WA
e-mail: info@smokestack-books.co.uk
www.smokestack-books.co.uk

Both
Steven Blyth
Cover image: Chris Hart
Author photograph: Steven Garrity

Printed by
EPW Print & Design Ltd

ISBN 978-0-9568144-3-2
Smokestack Books gratefully
acknowledges the support of
Arts Council England

Smokestack Books is
represented by Inpress Ltd
www.inpressbooks.co.uk

For my family

Acknowledgements

Acknowledgements are due to the editors of the following magazines, where some of these poems were first published: *Aesthetica, Acumen, Dreamcatcher, The Interpreter's House, Magma, Orbis, Other Poetry, PN Review, The Rialto, Seam, Smiths Knoll, The Spectator, Staple* and *Tears in the Fence*.

Contents

Name

A lot of people think that Captain Bligh
is an ancestor of mine. The surname
is similar, of course, but not the same.
I never correct them. I nod and smile.

He may be one of history's villains
but there's something exciting about him.
Unlike those I'm really descended from –
workers in factories, mills and mines.

No knights, captains of industry, colonels…
And so I play along, join in the jokes
about breadfruit and mutineers, and hope
my ancestors would forgive this betrayal,

wouldn't set me adrift in a lifeboat –
I know I'd never find my way home.

Staff Discount Card

Top brass? A director and his lad?
We'd see staff trying to suss me and dad

whenever we shopped in that menswear chain.
They didn't recognise my dad as one

who worked in a shop round here, didn't dare
ask, 'So what do you do?' He let them wonder

but was no boss. The card was gran's. She'd worked
sewing on buttons for years, the card a perk

she could carry into retirement,
dad the second holder she could nominate.

Always managers who helped dad and me.
They'd offer to throw in a tie for free,

alter dad's suits for half price, expedite
any orders. They called me *Sir* (I was eight).

We were so special and my gran loved
to hear those stories. She laughed and laughed.

Things were the opposite in her stories –
one of the lowest in those clothing factories,

least skilled, least paid, most at risk during lay-offs.
She never went near their ladies wear shops

where she could have made them fuss over her,
fooling them just like we did. Not once.
When she died we found her card in a drawer,

discarded amongst bits and bobs. And buttons.

Paul's Great Grandmother

Its clock tower appeared before the ads
on *Coronation Street*. We'd 'Ooo' as kids –

something we knew on the telly. She'd jeer,

wouldn't let us sit and eat a pie
on its steps like all our friends did. She'd eye

its Roman pillars like a Visigoth,

remind us how this impressive Town Hall
was built on the back of wealth from the mill,

tell us how the din left her half-deaf,

how a loom's workings took her uncle's hand.
They said her first love – her brother's best friend –

was crushed to death in a warehouse accident.

The one joy that came from it – reading lips,
the way to talk in there. She could gossip

through the window of a bus with a friend

who was queuing to board. She had stories
of swapping insults about mill owners

who were right by their side, inspecting. 'Clueless!'

Ninety, friends dead, she said, 'I've lived too long.'
The last speaker of a forgotten tongue

while the Town Hall stood there as grand as ever,

an illuminated capital letter
starting a fresh page. To those who knew her

it will always seem a little smudged.

Hobby

A set of golf clubs in the garden shed.

She bought them for his birthday when he retired.
They're like the bones of some beast that's died

from neglect. A couple of rounds. Not keen.

She tells him that he needs a hobby now,
says he's like a bad smell around the house,

wants him from under her feet, off her nerves.

She brings home brochures for the tech's night school,
a good pub guide, walking boots... She's hopeful

about the latest thing – some oil paints.

Something he used to do in his twenties.
She thinks, *landscapes – day trips with flask and butties.*

One effort from then hangs in the front room –

a stone bridge, some trees. A place they went courting.
'Take it up again,' she says. 'You could improve.'
He stares at it – the light and water wrong –

as though he's spotted a fake, lost a fortune.

Funeral

Birthdays, you'd send a card,
my three-million times removed aunt.
Things I didn't like on the front –
    steam trains, footballers, cars...
It's because you didn't know me.
We met at weddings. Twice. Briefly.

If you had known me well,
I doubt that we'd have got on –
me the atheist while you're one
    whose coffin's in the aisle
of the church you went to each day,
where they sing hymns with their arms raised.

Not grief but guilt I'm feeling –
I never sent a thank you note.
Thought you'd stop. Take the huff. *Spoilt brat!*
    But they kept on coming.
A surprise in the second post.
Your proof, perhaps, that God exists.

Inheritance

She's going from A to D, my aunt Val.
Like a note pitched to make the family howl

rather than a change in size. What a way
to spend what her dad – my granddad – left her.
Why not tasteful furniture like her sister
or, like her brother, sensibly saved?

She's blunt – 'I've always wanted bigger tits.'
Mid-fifties. Still time to flaunt them a bit.

Not that a flat chest ever proved a problem –
a queue of local lads when she was younger,
all eager to get inside her bra. Wonder
it didn't happen sooner, says my mum –

nineteen and pregnant with my eldest cousin.
The night she knew, her head went in the oven,

terrified of what my granddad would do –
disown her, have it adopted, kill the dad…
He found her just in time. Did none of that.
I think of her now, so bruised she can't move;

remember what she said about that night –
'My dad hugged me so hard it hurt.'

The Family

A cuppa in it at my grandparents –
the ride to school often left me frozen.
I'd lock up my bike in their back garden,
their house just two minutes walk from the gates.

Free from their social club, it commemorated
the Silver Jubilee in '77.
Half–mug size with a portrait of the Queen.
Odd they should keep it, I thought. Both hated

the Royal Family, famous in our family
for shouting abuse at them in the papers
and on TV – 'Bunch of bloody scroungers!
And they say we live in a democracy!'

They started my own hatred of things royal.
One morning, I asked them why they'd kept it.
They said because it held the right amount
for a twelve year old slurping against the bell.

One of my cousins took it when they'd died.
She collects that stuff, said it meant they really
had a soft spot for the monarchy,
stuck it on a shelf in her front room's shrine

between a coronation plate and spoon.
At Christmas and on birthdays, I visit,
think of the real reason. The Queen smiles down
as if to acknowledge our little secret

and suddenly, I'm warm inside again.

The Seafarers

Cockles for my sister and me. A treat
for the Saturday nights when dad took mum
to some working mens' club where she'd sing,
grandma babysitting us. He'd buy them
from our town's big, famous fish market. Puzzling –
no rivers round here and miles from the beach.

Though on such nights it seemed they crossed an ocean,
those clubs in places that, at eight years old,
were as remote as a foreign land.
Wigan, Burnley, Leigh. Once as far as Sheffield.
Once, overnight in Wales. A star in demand,
that was those long journeys' explanation.

She topped a few bills, performed on the radio.
While she sang, I had TV's Palladium –
Shirley Bassey, Cilla Black and Lulu.
I'd imagine the same applause for mum,
same cries for more, same flowers they threw...
Sometimes, I'd beg them to let me go,

desperate to see her sing. They said, 'Too young.'
By the time I'd reached an age when I guess
they'd have allowed me to tag along,
she'd given up. In her wardrobe, that dress,

long and silver-sequined – a mermaid's tail.

Secret Agent

I thought my dad was a secret agent.
Manilla envelopes would arrive marked
On Her Majesty's Service. Like the title
of that Bond film. The word secret was missed
but who cares when you're ten, watching him bent,
night after night, over a drawing table,

doing plans for his MI5 masters.
He'd dismantle dividers and compass,
clip them in a box placed out of my reach.
Gadgets from Q Division? Most suspicious,
the way he'd tell me and my sister
not to mention this work out on our street.

All that hush hush stuff was down to the tax –
declared little of what he earned on
Her Majesty's forms, worried about snitching
nosey neighbours. A day job draughtsman
drawing plans on the side – granny flats,
conservatories, extensions to kitchens...

It paid for holidays and Christmas presents,
for a birthday party clown or conjuror.
All those evenings and weekends he spent
earning that bit extra for us. I wonder
if he resented it then or still resents,
thinking of all the other dads who went

down to the pub, the match, the golf club?
'No. Course not. Don't be daft,' he'll say if asked.
But changes subject, unwilling to be pushed,
as if bound by some official secrets act.

Glider

It happened to two kids in my school year.
One boy's dad went to work away, returned
rarely; eventually never. The other
left for his younger and childless secretary.
And there was the dad of my cousin's friend
and the dad of the twins at number three…

It makes me think of that glider kit.
It was a surprise brought home by my dad
one ordinary Tuesday evening. A gift
I never questioned, as didn't my sister
the big doll he got her. We were just glad
to have them. More and more now, I wonder –

was it down to some sudden urge – *Treat them!* –
or because of guilt for angry moments
we'd forgotten? But that wasn't like him –
gifts were for birthdays, Christmas, a reward.
Or was it an apology for thoughts
about walking out like those others had?

I could ask, of course, but know he'd stay hush
if that was the reason behind those gifts,
unable to hurt me by owning up
to ever hating life with us. The glider
was a good one. Must have cost him a bit.
It soared, seemed to stay up forever.

Tricks of the Trade

A friend's dad was in the Magic Circle,
performed his tricks at parties now and then.
We asked how they were done? He couldn't tell.
Sworn secrets. Maddening when you're ten.

One Saturday afternoon, his mum out,
we told his dad we were off to the park,
crept back and peeked through the front room's door-crack,
hoping to see him there with a top hat

training pets to sit squashed and still in it,
checking levitating hoops, loaded dice,
secret doors in a magic cabinet...
Instead, a briefcase and work from his office.

Seeing that was like watching a failed trick,
those invoices like playing cards tumbling
from up his sleeves. How disappointing,
him as boring as any other clerk.

Later, that friend got me an invite
to the kids' Christmas do at his dad's firm.
He did his act – turned a black rabbit white,
made cut ropes join, coins appear in his palm...

The finale, a vanishing cockatiel.
If he'd known what we'd seen that Saturday,
known what we'd felt and thought of him, I'd say
he'd want to make all that vanish as well –

some mind-trick so we couldn't remember.
No chance. Such stuff too tough for the amateur.

First Cigarette

I was nine, that's all. A Lambert & Butler
belonging to our chain-smoking neighbour,

Mrs O'Connor, who once babysat
for me and my younger sister. That night

she blew smoke rings for us. Large ones, drifting
slowly across the front room; or a string

of speeding smaller ones; or large with small
blown through it. Like magic. We were in awe.

Wanting to do the same, sister tucked in
and her making a cuppa, I sucked on

one she'd left half–finished and glowing
in the ashtray she'd brought. Green and gasping,

that's how she found me. She laughed that laugh
of hers that turned into a dreadful cough.

She promised she wouldn't tell mum and dad.
I worried she might, this secret best shared

with those my own age on some street corner.
I heard her cough too often that summer –

in her garden or as she walked by our house.
It was that secret trying to get out,

her adult urge to tell getting stronger.
Worse and worse. Soon, 'She's with us no longer,'

my dad said. Safe now. Glad instead of sad,
and I felt no guilt at feeling glad.

It was just like more of her magic –
some spectacular vanishing trick.

The Ball Boy

He couldn't kick or throw a ball straight.
Couldn't hit one at all. Or bowl. Or catch.
Useless. We never let him have a touch,
picked him last for teams playing on our street.

Then suddenly he turned brave. He'd volunteer
to get the ball when it went into gardens
that made the rest of us feel sick with fear –
those of old men rumoured to have shotguns,

the old lady who looked like a witch.
He'd dart in and dodge the huge dog we'd heard
had killed several postmen. He had the nerve
for the mad man's long grass and the long search.

Picking teams, he was then one of the first.
Kept sweet. We'd pass to him or let him bat.
Once, let him take a penalty (he missed).
When it went too high and far he'd get it.

Not bitten. Not shot. No tail from the witch.
Triumphant. His goal. His six. His howzat!
He'd then throw it back to where it moved so fast
and struck so hard, could hurt so much.

Christmas, 1979

A big fuss among us older children
when we heard he was to be Father Christmas
at the party for Sunday School's infants.
For years the job had been Mr. Flint's.
His death that summer gave this creep the chance,
part of his new position as church warden.

The older girls would point and whisper, 'Watch!'
His hands ran the length of each little girl
he'd playfully lift. He was always keen
to chase as the 'cuddles monster' or squeeze
'to warm them up' in that cold church hall.
Big girls knew what his hands would quickly touch.

One even had a story of a friend
who remembered a Brownies trip to the pool –
him in there! Places his fingers had gone!
Some of the adults caught wind of that one –
'Filthy rumours! Affectionate, that's all.
No children of his own. He's caring, kind.'

We watched the little girls sit on his knee
to get their gift. His hand stroked their backs,
moved towards their bums. Dangerously close.
The vicar was there and some of those
on our church's committee. Laughter, jokes.
They ate mince pies and had a small sherry.

Being older, they allowed us a sip,
like that first communion wine on our lips,
this taste just as big a shock – burning, tingling,
something given to deaden the tongue.

The Leavers' Do

My niece, in her first year at my old school,
says they have nothing like it now. The stories
a constant request from her and her friends.
A local Italian place for a meal
on the last Friday of the last term.
Few went, keen to be rid of the place
earlier in the day. It didn't help
that the real bastards on the staff would come,

spoil this as they had the past five years.
Like Gibson, who hurled board dusters at you,
lifted you from your chair by your hair.
Or Miss Houghton, who refused to hear
excuses; Fridays, kept the whole class back.
Still, worth it that night to see alcohol
like beauty's kiss on the beast's lips – the lot
made foolish or more friendly than they'd like.

Gibson fawning over Katie Meacher,
pawing her, trying to smooch in the bar;
Miss Houghton telling the dirtiest jokes.
The best was Mr Glick, the physics teacher,
as grey and scary as one of his steel rods
raised as if to strike. He had to be helped
to the taxi and puked up on the way.
It's such great fun for my niece and her friends,

many of those nasty ones still there.
I think of my stories getting round,
some plucky kid – 'Do you remember, sir...?'
I smile. Some huge hangover starts to clear.

Teachers' Houses

We kept our ears to the school playground,
Dave Jones and me. Rumours of home addresses –
a kid whose gran lived nearby or some friend
who'd spotted one out front cutting the grass.

Come weekend, we'd cycle over. Wonderful
how there we saw stuff that made them laughable

these people who filled our reports with Ds,
our books with crosses, made us come back later
for re-tests. We'd watch their houses patiently,
certain we'd soon be aching with laughter –

Mrs Brown's weird husband with his huge beard;
Mr Peel up a ladder looking scared;

Mrs McAndrew's stupid sausage dog.
Funniest, Mr Gibson's teenage daughter
yelling at him on the porch, 'Fucking sod!
You can't tell me what I can and can't wear!'

Nothing at Mr Watts' to raise a smile.
Huge. Immaculate. A swimming pool.

A silver sports model second car
parked on the drive. We saw his girlfriend,
as beautiful as any movie star,
kiss him in the window, then draw the blind.

All much worse because he was the cruellest.
Harsh marker, returned tests in order from first

to last, making you stand till you got yours.
Still, we were soon laughing again – threw stones
from bushes and smashed back lights on both cars.
But silent, yards apart while cycling home

like those 'test conditions' they'd insist upon,
and knowing we'd just failed another one.

Baby

Our rations of hope running low,
the pregnancy test's blue line
was like land on the horizon.
It's a simile that still holds
now that he's here – this time our past
feels like the far-off coast,

so distant because we know
it will be just history for him.
Her smile when I mention this to mum
says that we're where all parents go.
Trying to cope with his colic
makes it seem we arrived by shipwreck,

are struggling to build a shelter
in the middle of the storm.
We notice now our parents' hands – so worn.
Your dad says, 'These days mine bruise easier.'
He shows us his latest one.
It sits on his palm – this new country's coin.

The Smack

Seconds after it, hugs and 'Sorry, sorry'
poured from me like handfuls of bribing toffees.
Red marks on my son's arm. I'd broken my vow.
His toddlers' tantrum did it and now
I'm guilt-ridden in my Town Hall office,
worrying he'll never forgive me.

In the ballroom, the weekly tea dance starts,
the antique Wurlitzer sending tunes
drifting through the building – brisk, jolly tempos
of military two–steps, gay gordons, tangos.
Then, as these over-seventies eat their scones,
I've Got a Lovely Bunch of Coconuts.

Something to cheer me from that generation,
as if it says my smack wasn't so bad –
We did it all the time; some gave the strap.
But our kids still love us. True, perhaps.
Take my granddad – often cuffing my dad
who has one story of near concussion.

But when he got frail, dad still cared for him –
brought meals at weekends, arranged the home help,
cleaned up when he had trouble 'down below.'
I'd do it for my parents even though
they clipped my ears, gave my legs the odd slap.
The music plays on, soundtrack to a film,

a comedy, of course, making life
a *Carry On*, the sort in which characters
chortle, chuckle, guffaw, giggle or titter,
but never really laugh.

Both

It's Sunday morning in the park. My son
is riding his new bike. I'm relaxing
on a bench. We're both having a good time.
A thrill for both of us this first real spin
without stabilisers. Both of us laughing
at any dog that tries to catch him.
No chance! Both of us treating like treasure
conkers he's found. A good time for sure.

But enough, I wonder, to earn its place
in both our memories when he's older?
With my own parents, I too often find
only they or I recall. Like the Christmas
I ate my sister's selection box. Laughter
from them. I just shrug. They're equally blind
to my memory of my mother's shriek
when the neighbours' cat killed a grass snake.

I sit here feeling sad that this moment
might only be shared now, could be a blank
to one of us in years to come. Sadness
made worse when I see him so distant,
peddling on the other side of the park,
as distant as failed memory might make us.
Sadness soon gone, though, when he stops his bike
to look for me and waves and I wave back.

Carrying My Son

He's six. Asleep. Head on my shoulder. Heavy.
A pain in my upper back as I walk
along the seafront to our B & B.
I'm gasping like I did on the beach
chasing the ball. Unfit. The car to work,
fry-ups for breakfast and large chips for lunch.

This pain could easily be one in my chest,
the heart attack that does in slobs like me.
Though my heart seems stronger – in love at least –
since he and his younger sister were born.
So strong I wish, *Me, not them* at each story
about cancers or a new viral strain.

Some might take a more scientific view –
vital that we want to further our kind,
love nature's trick to make sure that we do.
Their evidence is strong from what I can tell.
Then I think of this resort's fairground –
hoopla, duck hook, rifle range. Tricks as well.

They make them look easy to lure you in.
I fall for it. Sometimes, though, I win.

White Noise

The sound of clouds whispering to each other.
That's how I explain the tranny's static
to my young son. I know what causes it
but have no time to explain, more bothered

about the noise from his sister. New born.
A feed? A nappy change? Since she arrived
he's been demanding, has often misbehaved –
jealousy we were told to prepare for.

The only thing that keeps him quiet,
that tranny. The tuner fascinates him.
Verse from Blondie… shhh… chorus from The Jam…
shhh… some news headlines… shhh… an ad for carpets…

Later I find him listening only
to the static, as if to their whispers
to glean experience in cloudly matters
like being out of reach, wandering lonely…

Steps

Just one achievement
from your feet so far –
kicking into touch
'late developer.'
Nearly two. Five steps
the best you've managed.
Today it's more tests
at the hospital,
talk of hip problems
an op might fix. *Might!*
What if it doesn't?
We'll cope, we feel sure,
love you just the same.
What parent wouldn't?

Home, we keep trying,
count and hope – 1, 2,
3, 4, 5... you fall.
Later, we're shopping.
Unfolding the pram
is too much trouble,
so I carry you.
Light. Once. Bigger now,
my arms start to ache.
We take turns. *Burden.*
There it is – the word
we've tried not to think.
We can fall as well.
And much, much further.

Bedtime

My nine year old son has broken a glass.

He was making some pop while I put
his six year old sister to bed. He cut

his thumb but didn't cry or come for me,

knows our secret's out if he does. He creeps
down after my fake, 'Night, night. Time to sleep,'

gets extra TV. When my wife works late

it's easier this way. Story and tuck in
one at a time so there's no competition

for my attention. It's a lazy way

that leaves me worried about bad examples –
deception and lies acceptable.

Worried he'll end up one of those laughed at

pathological types who says he flew
fighter planes, is a black-belt in jujitsu,

slept with a supermodel… Or worse

a conman or fraudster that I'll disown
or even grow to hate… Soon, I'm back down

tidying up glass. He says his thumb stings.

I ask if he wants it kissed better. 'No!'
He's big and brave. Moments later it's, 'Yes,'
as if we make a blood-pact when I do

to keep love and honesty between us.

The Black Arts

A full moon on the night
that I wrote down backwards
the questions I wanted
for my third year exams;
folded the sheet six times,
burnt it in the meths flame

of my chemistry set,
kept the ashes bottled
in my blazer's pocket.
My own spell based on stuff
picked up in library books
on witchcraft. Crazy. Dumb.

But swotting hadn't helped
and I was so desperate
not to get Ds again,
not to sob in the loos,
bottom of the class, scared
I'd move down. Names. Sniggers.

I couldn't wait to leave.
My son can't wait to start.
A few one-day visits –
loves the little library,
the computer corner,
bright numbers and letters

hanging in the windows.
I take a photograph
of him in his neat tie,
white shirt, grey shorts, shined shoes.
To capture his big day.
But also to capture

that keen, confident smile
of these few years before

Turn over and begin,
answer all the questions...
Incantations to turn
a prince into a frog.

Floorboard

Worried that it might wake the kids
we step over it – the creak
like an opening coffin lid
in one of their nightmares that break

our precious adult hours. Time spent
giving them reassuring hugs
costs us talk of how the day went,
a chapter, TV, making love...

Sometimes I think of a friend's dad
who went mad if his lad got up.
We were eight. Once, his legs all red.
That night's TV, some tie in the cup.

Now our kids are with their aunt.
Blackpool. The plan, we join them today.
White lies on the phone – 'Car's conked out.
You'd better bring them back Sunday.'

Another night of sex downstairs,
the pub till late, music played loud.
But we still step over that board,
as if now scared that friend's dad will stir.

March

A Land Rover flashing to turn right
against the school-run tail back at the lights.

Thick snow on the bonnet and roof, the stuff
my kids dreamed of all winter, wanting so much

a snowman on our lawn. It never came –
just thin falls that didn't stick, like today's.

That Land Rover must be from on the hills.
The big houses. A friend's dad once filled

a truck he took up there with snow. Odd
to see that snowman in their small, bare yard –

some out-of-place butler of newly made
millionaires. If they had been, you could say

his dad earned every penny – aching back,
frost-bitten fingers, the truck getting stuck...

But we were still jealous. A gang of us
kicked it to powder, trampled it to slush.

Shameful stuff I won't admit to my two,
keen to show them the right thing. Like now,

hoping, from the back seat, they watch and learn
as I, politely, let the Land Rover turn.

Some snow falls from its roof into the road.
'Look! Look!' I yell, as if it's my reward.

Game

After my third thrashing on his Playstation
I see his hands fake fumbles and go slow
on the controller. He lets me win now,
just as I have let him win so often –

that fatherly thing of serving him one
that's a doddle to return, shooting low
so he's sure to save it, aiming a throw
to miss the stumps so he can make the run.

'Why go easy on me?' I say. He shrugs,
then laughs awkwardly and starts to redden.
'Because you're crap,' he manages to mumble.

What did I expect? I know love's the reason.
Asking a boy to speak about such things
as unfair as a fast over-arm ball.

Portrait

For Amelia Hart

When it comes to drawing, your dad's the best
I've known. The photo he e-mailed to me
of you just minutes old, was like a sketch
he might have done when we were in our teens,

stuff from the covers of prog-rock albums –
griffons, dragons, you the wet-haired mer-child
from some *Yes* concept LP's gate-fold.
As fantastical a creature, it seems,

as impossible for you to exist –
parents pushing forty, shrugging when asked
if they fancied a family. 'It just
hasn't happened.' That's that. Uncle and aunt.

A world that wasn't expecting you feels
your presence – you break its pots, scratch its woodwork,
stain it with spills. On its face, a surprised look
you capture in your scribble on its walls.

Saying the Usual Stuff

A chance meeting in Asda's car park.
I say the usual stuff – like how he's grown,
how he's the spit of his mum. She worked on
my team before deciding to chuck work,
wanting to spend more time with her son.

The morning he was born, our office heard
about problems – a caesarean,
irregular heartbeat, resuscitation.
Till we were sure of his breath, ours was held.
We pushed back heavy tomb-door thoughts of Ann

from Personnel – went full term and lost it.
Later, we learnt how close to that it came.
If it had, how different seeing her today.
Crushing grief, perhaps, the reason she quit
and me crouching behind cars, feeling ashamed

because suddenly I can't bear to face
that kind of usual stuff – 'Thinking of you.
So sorry. If there's anything we can do.'
So inadequate in such a case.
So far from when it's gran at ninety-two.

Still, that didn't happen and I can say
'Nice when they're sleeping through. Any teeth yet?
By now, my first could stand up in his cot.'
It makes me feel that the world is OK.
Better than hiding, knowing that it's not.

Crime

I'm working late again. My friends snap, 'Don't!'
They make it seem as bad as stealing from
the petty cash, fiddling a mileage claim…
The one about home being most important.

Travelling back, I think of my dad's defence
when we moaned that his hours were too long.
He'd say, 'It pays for *this* and *this* and *this*…'
On every *this*, his finger would prod something –

a toy that had been the 'big' Christmas present,
the calendar on which we'd ringed our hols,
TV, settee, armchair, even the walls,
windows, curtains. It was like an attempt

to put his fingerprints on everything
so as to prove he'd been here all along.

Telephone

My mum told me to 'keep quiet, sit still.'
She turned the TV down. A phone call

from someone on the late shift for my dad.
He wasn't to be disturbed or distracted

when taking such calls. Strange to hear him
using work-words, the 'Hiya' of home

replaced with things like, 'I'll *attend* to it,'
and *regarding* this or *regarding* that,

'Yes, it's *essential*.' Once or twice, a '*Sir*.'
It helped me in my first job years later –

they said I was excellent on the phone.
Good early appraisals. I faltered though

when asked if I felt the post was for me,
how I saw my future at the company?

In truth, I was only there because dad
had insisted I get a job. I'd planned

a lazy summer after those last exams.
But dad brought home application forms.

'Get a job! Anything at all!' he said
with such urgency, as if work itself

was a ringing phone that I had to answer
and take my turn to say *attend, regarding, sir…*

Back Page

'Buy a newspaper and read the back page.'
My stint of fifth form work experience
and dad had sussed out I was bored witless.
It was the only advice that he gave.

I loathed sport but he said, 'A useful thing
to start a chat with, make friends.' He taught me
a way of getting through the drudgery
of three weeks of photocopies and filing –

discussions about some dirty cropper
the blind ref missed, a clever off-side trap,
the thrashing of a big club in the cup
by lower or even non-league no-hopers.

He'd suggest I bought one from the news stand
when dropping me off at the bus station
on his own journey into work, often
pressing some money into my hand,

the closest he's come to being classical –
coins for Charon, easing my way to hell.

Horror Films

We would discuss our favourite Hammer classic,
agreed about *The Ring* – the remake

not half as scary as the Japanese

original. You thought video nasties
had charms, especially those from the mid-80s

like *Driller Killers 2*. Our love of them

filled almost every lunchtime and teabreak,
as if the dreary office paperwork

was blood-splattered, shocking us out of

our half-asleep day. It lasted a year,
then I got a job somewhere else. Soon after

you did the same. A few pints, some e–mails,

then we lost touch. Years now. Our shared passion
for those films wasn't enough on its own.

We needed more than the power of

Dracula, Wolfman or the Mummy's Curse.
We needed the power of file, invoice,

fax, paperclip… Such dull ordinary stuff

we don't notice its influence on our lives,
dismissing it like that strange noise outside,

the one we tell ourselves is just the wind.

Junior

Mr Gilchrist was one of the 'big' bosses.
A director. Rarely seen. Epilepsy
meant that he couldn't drive. Occasionally,
the one car-owning junior in the office,
I would be told to give him lifts to meetings
being held in the firm's other building.

If you were given that job you were warned
never to put music on in the car.
Doing so could damage your career.
That's what once happened, everyone reckoned.
The story was some clerk had lost out on
his dead cert of a promotion

because he played a *Clash* cassette. Gilchrist
said, 'Not my cup of tea.' Frowned. Turned it down.
'It can't be true,' I'd sometimes say. 'The man
seems nice enough to me.' During those lifts
he'd ask how I was getting on at work,
talk about his family, tell the odd joke.

But older colleagues said, 'Son, heed the warning.'
So music stayed off. And I drove with care –
another tip they gave me. I made sure
to check my mirrors before turning,
brake gently and in good time, watch my speed,
keep well over to my side of the road.

Lefty Robot

A colleague calls me that. He knows I'll strike
even though I'm against it, of the view
it won't get us the pay increase. 'You
do what the Union tells you to.' He's right –

it's as if my shop steward great granddad
snuck me into his factory while asleep,
put cogs and pistons in me that pump
and turn to make me do what he did.

And so I do my shift on the picket.
Two days later it breaks. We're sent back in.
And yet I feel such satisfaction.
Family honour? Loyalty to my past?

It's hard to know exactly but seems
as well as control me, those parts can gleam.

Dress Down Day

On the Town Hall's tiled floors, our trainers squeak
sounding like excited small dogs yapping.
It fits the good mood we're in this morning
because, for once, we can wear what we like.

Well worth the pound to the mayor's charity
to shed sober suits or sensible skirts.
At lunchtime we chat about when we first
had to wear suits for work. The same story –

we hated it. Boring black and drab greys
or navy that looks like black. And too formal.
It wasn't us. But in the end we all
got used to goodbye to ourselves each day

in the mirror – fastening that top button,
straightening ties, brushing down pin-striped shoulders.
Today, so many T-shirts are worn.
They're like the kind people buy as souvenirs

because they want to remember somewhere,
perhaps one day return, settle there.

Castaway

I am thinking about the roles we'd take
if we were marooned on a desert island.
Bill from accountancy would build the shelters –
loves DIY. Ian from PR looks like
the sort would could protect us from predators –
big, sporty. Such thoughts keep me entertained

during boring meetings. This one's about
'Corporate Strategy and Performance.'
I should pay attention but never do.
Instead, wonder who's done drugs or work out
the percentage of life spent on the loo
or put people's ties in order of preference…

Today, they each make points and ask a question.
My thoughts would appal them; they'd want me hung
from the highest bar on their mid-year graph,
would agree with the teacher who'd yell, 'Listen
or you'll never amount to much in life!'
Often aimed at me, at the back, daydreaming.

They're right. Listening would have got me further,
got me where I am faster. I try to.
Try now. Try hard. But within minutes it's
who'd hunt, who'd grow the crops, who'd find fresh water?
The thought I could pay attention to this
as hopeless as my plan to get us rescued.

Promotion

'It's an offer you can't refuse.' A joke

from my department's director. It felt
as though I'd really joined the mob, management

almost as feared and hated. They can sink

your earnings in a concrete overcoat;
left a P45 for some poor bloke

on his desk to be found in the morning,

as shocking as that horse's head in bed;
and when it comes to their meetings, what's said

is governed by their own kind of omertà.

I told myself I wouldn't be like them –
was relaxed when someone stretched their lunchtime

just beyond the hour, when I suspected

a sickie was thrown or they'd used the phone
for personal calls… Even when I was told

'Kath's due her final warning for lateness'

I vowed to go easy on her, be nice.
First it was, 'This is hard for both of us…

I know your mum's been ill… We'll work this out…'

Then it was, 'But the rules are the rules…
You must understand… And if it continues…'

Weeks later, a mob hitman on TV.

They asked him about his methods. He said,
'First, one to the heart; then, one to the head.'

Married to the Job

A phrase I've often heard where I work.
Said of Bill Cox who begged not to retire,
died within a year of doing so. Said
of Peter Boardman, the over-time king,
screamed by his wife at the reception desk
the day she left him. Said of Janet Squires
who worried about the firm's overspending
and sent her nerves plunging into the red.

My only vow – that's not how I'll end up.
And that's why I am not going back
to switch off my PC. Done for the weekend,
I've left a spread-sheet on screen, unsaved,
at risk from cleaners or a power blip.
I could lose the lot. A full day's work.
Important. But work's not my wife. Instead
I'll treat it like those teenage girlfriends –

are we serious, going steady? No.
'See you Monday,' then not give it a thought
while I enjoy the weekend's precious hours.
When I get back to my desk, it's there, untouched.
I click *save* – like the casual kiss hello
I'd give those girls. I remember how it
always felt too eager, filled with too much
relief at seeing them, told them, *I'm all yours.*

Murder

A meeting... *there's blood all over the place...*
taking calls... *knife still in her...* filing away
some notes... *eyes so white against her red face...*
I make mistakes, people ask, 'You OK?'

A forensic shot of a murder scene.
It appears in the police training handbooks
that they're copying in reprographics.
New work that pays well and by the afternoon

I'm drafting targets, a twelve month strategy,
instructed to get more of this income.
As the dull task preoccupies me
I forget her. Killed for a second time –

among harmless rulers and rubber bands
stalks boredom with his big bare hands.

Clock

I've told my kids my job's to bang the bell
on the Town Hall clock. What else can you tell

a three and five year old who think it looks

exciting – a rocket, Rapunzel's tower?
The bureaucracy I'm up to in there

is hard to explain – it could be God,

death or the facts of life if it weren't so dull,
a dullness that's best hidden by this tale

that thrills them whenever they hear it chime.

I never hear it when I'm in the office;
even mid-day's twelve can go unnoticed –

too immersed in the work that leaves me grumpy

when I get home; too tired to play with them,
longing for when they're in bed. Only then

do I sometimes hear it in the distance –

out late in the garden on a summer night.
It's like the call of some huge, lonely beast.

The Bomb

A gun down there, that's what everyone said.
To shoot those crazy from being locked in
or give a coup de grâce to any wounded.
Under the first Town Hall I worked in,

a concrete bunker for a select few
who'd run the borough after the nukes.
One day, some of us were allowed to view
the 'control room.' Phones, cabinets and desks –

a dull office, the world to be rebuilt
by filling in some forms, making some calls.
And yet scary. They were ready for it.
Expecting it? Scariest of all,

the map on the wall. People found their road.
What did that red pin mean? That blue sticker?
A certain death? No chance? Our stomachs churned.
A hint of fallout in the air down there.

Thoughts of the gun, though, still excited us.
Where was it? In that locked cabinet or drawer?
We wandered the room hoping we were close.
Getting warmer. Warmer. Red hot. On fire.

The Prison

The power station's site, that's where it stands.
A place that once warmed these boroughs
now chills them – thoughts that escapees might hijack
a train that's stopped at the signals, the line
running within five-hundred yards of the grounds;
or want wallets like a western's masked robbers;
or some serial killer might wreck the track,
hoping to make up for all that lost time.

Perhaps a plan to make punishment worse –
freedom hurtling past their barred windows.
Cruellest, the service to the airport or match
or those on bank hols with an extra carriage.
Well worth our worries about the place
to know each trip we make gets back at those
who'd mug or burgle us, shoplift, bag snatch.
Good to think they're doing staler porridge.

Perhaps instead it's an attempt at reform.
Tutors point at the commuters' 7.30 –
Look. Learn. There go people who are honest
to honest jobs for honest pay. Join them.
Start by catching their train the day you're free.
And buy a ticket. This is your first test.

Remember to do it as they do – grudgingly.

Prosperity

The street sign says just that.
Not *Prosperity Street*

or *way* or *close* or *road*.
Less a name for this narrow

dirt track cul-de-sac,
more a description. *Look*

no further – here it is.
It winds behind some semis.

Neat lawn, conservatory,
patio... *Prosperity*.

Traces of cobble stone
under the mud. So old.

It makes you wonder – once
did it lead somewhere else?

Working Life

for Jim Burns

We're laughing about the times
we've skived off from our various jobs.
Your greatest achievement
was forty odd years ago
taking your time, detours and the long
way round while delivering the army's mail
in Germany. My best was months
of faking errands to Manchester
after working out no one at the firm
asked or noticed what a junior was doing.
We feel proud of it because it means
we've never taken work too seriously,
and let it grind us down, take us over.
It leads me to tell you about
the time I caught Rachel in *Typing*
reading a Jackie Collins novel
from inside her open desk drawer.
I told her to carry on
but maybe try something better next time –
Hemingway, Kerouac, Joyce.
You say, 'There's a poem there.'
I agree and say, 'You can have that one.'
You tell me it's mine, I insist it's all yours.
We pass it to each other for a while –
pretending we can skive off that job too.

Dolls House

We found it in the loft of our new house,

its pipe-cleaner family bearing big grins.
A good omen, we thought, us determined

to make this place a happier home.

Never to slam its doors in anger, sulk
in its garden, stomp up its stairs, lock

its loo door and cry behind it for hours...

We blamed the old place for that. Bad area.
It set our nerves on edge – a drug dealer,

the neighbours' music booming, joy riders...

Here is better. Quieter. A tree-lined street.
Confetti to celebrate our new start,

we agreed when we first saw its pink blossom.

We buy the dolls' house replica furniture,
restore the roof and windows. It's our daughter's

big Christmas present. On Boxing Day

our son's Star Wars figures invade. Lasers
and light sabres. Battling tentacled monsters.

A touch of realism for the place.

Cheese

From the kids' smiles on the snaps, you can't tell –
wide and toothy on ponies, by the pool,

on the hired bikes... All taken in great weather.
In truth, the worst hols we've ever had.

You'd decided to reduce your dose
then come off completely. Slowly, of course.

'Like a balloonist losing altitude
to land,' you said. Seems you misjudged that last

few feet again. A fall that's far enough
to break bones. Or kill. When you raised that knife

I thought you might – scariest moment
among routine yelling and slamming doors.

I calmed it down. The kids cowered and cried.
I lied to them that you were just tired. Lied

to myself that all the times like these
haven't left love as un–repairable

as the chalet's plate you hurled at the wall.
And lie now to those who ask if it went well –

'A great time. Look at these.' Proof for them
in the kids' smiles. 'Say cheese,' I'd say to them.

'Come on now, say cheese.' Cheese. The kind that stinks.

Serious

'They met during family holidays and fell in love.'
(BBC News)

They're fourteen year old runaways

whose families didn't approve.
Third item on the evening news

and in our office the next day

a joke: 'Give them ten years together
and they'll be running from each other.'

They're silly. Everyone agrees,

guesses they've given the daft gifts
that everyone gives at first –

big fluffy bears, the single rose,

padded cards, love heart shaped chocs...
We laugh at how soon all that stops.

Do they think it's going to last?

Perhaps they have more of a chance
having heard some news reader announce

they've fallen in love, so straight-faced.

Landmark

Jill once admitted she was still in love

with her ex-husband, would go back tomorrow
despite being divorced ten years ago.

The office felt embarrassed for her, thinking

How pathetic she can't get over it,
as if she'd shown us some soppy love note,

the teenage sort that started their romance.

It seems almost certain she still reads them
on lonely nights in. All that love for him

and nothing she can do with it, her heart

holding it back like some enormous dam –
the kind of thing upon which the lost come,

then know exactly where they are.

Quiz Night

You were the first girl I kissed properly;

I was your first boy. You're back on business
and I'm here for a pint with the office

who are soon gone, leaving us to catch up –

our jobs, our kids, and those days' mutual friends.
Soon we're as silent as the snug's married ones,

as relieved when it starts, talk easy now –

about who's stayed longest at No. 1,
how many Oscars Star Wars won,

last year's winner of the Grand National...

Why prolong this? Now, nothing in common.
Polite excuses are a better option –

for me, the kids; for you, an early meeting.

But we stick it out until it's last orders
before saying goodbye. As if the answer

to why we've been sitting here for so long
might come if we give it enough time.
As if it's on the tip of our tongues.

Stupidity

Dad before that first holiday with friends –

'Precautions! Don't do anything stupid!'
Sixteen and just sex on my mind, I did –

a girl called Claire in the dunes. Advice ignored

like once before during the hols. 'Brake.
Don't drag your feet.' I was eight. A hired bike.

Downhill, I scuffed my shoes and hit a wall.

I wouldn't brake on this ride too. Nor her.
No precautions for a frenzied first timer!

Later, worries she'd be pregnant left me

feeling just as stupid as when dad showed
snaps of my 'crash' holiday – broken nose,

and black eyes on every one. They still trigger

the stories about all the stupid stuff
holiday freedom has made me do –   stuck

up a tree, swimming too far, trapped by tides...

Kept with the two snaps I have of Claire,
is the letter she sent two weeks later.
It contains our cleverly-coded all clear.

Witness

'As he was cycling to work he saw her speaking to another man
on her doorstep. He remembers this well because she was smiling
at the man and he wished she had been smiling at him instead.
He had admired her from afar each day.'
(Crimewatch)

He wishes now the bastard had been obvious,
like a black-hatted bad guy in a Western,
some clue that would have made him suspicious.
He imagines himself like John Wayne

striding up her path – 'This man botherin' you ma'am?'
Instead, he'd be TV's have-a-go hero.
He imagines her wishing for the same
as those hands tightened around her throat.

But she was smiling and so on he rode,
gave just a glance at who they think did it.
Height? Age? Not much he can tell the detective.

All that's clear is her smile – warm and wide,
the sort given to those you like. Or love?
That thought sits in his brain like a bullet.

Greasby's

They're one of the official auctioneers
of unclaimed lost baggage. He had bid there,
showed me a catalogue: *Black trolley case –
contains a watch, calculator, sportswear…*

*Holdall – contains 'laughing Buddha' statuettes,
toiletries, menswear (formal and leisure)…*
Each bag like a fairy tale's giant fish
that's gutted to reveal its swallowed treasure.

I said that I'd be bothered by the thought
some people might still miss their lost things,
just hadn't known how or where to reclaim
their favourite toy or heirloom ring,

a pain pulsing out like radar – *I want
it back, I want it back, I want it back…*
He told me I thought far too much,
should stop worrying about stuff like that.

'You can get some really good gear,' he said.
'Like these trainers.' To prove their perfect fit
he shuffled, tip-toed and stamped – showing off
a dance beyond my thinking two left feet.

Maggie

Thank you very very much, Margaret Thatcher,
for mass unemployment in the mid-80s.
It meant I couldn't follow my granddads,
dad and uncles into the jobs they had –
welders, plumbers, or working in factories
as a skilled operator or a fitter.

It meant I stumbled into education –
further, then higher – as 'something to do.'
I found philosophy, literature, art,
and read and wrote stuff I never thought
myself capable of. All thanks to you.
My life enriched. A sort of 'wealth creation.'

When it comes to those men, you'll find no thanks.
You're loathed for crushing their trades and industry.
I was pitied because I was 'unskilled,'
was like a child suddenly made disabled
in some accident you'd caused. Eventually
they laughed at me because I couldn't fix

a pipe or re-wire things or mend machines.
And I got intellectually superior
because they hadn't heard of Hume or Kant,
so they thought me a useless smart-arsed runt,
a gulf opening up as wide as your
North/South divide the obituary mentions.

The moment I heard you'd died, I was surprised
to find I gave a good riddance, 'Hooray!'
Realised those men would have cheered as well.
Suddenly, some bond between us as durable
as their rivets, solders and welds. That day
Britain's manual skills base seemed very much alive.